W9-ACM-889

Pioneer Spirit
The
Westward
Expansion

THE OREGON TRAIL

Rachel Lynette

PowerKiDS
press.
New York

For Claire

Published in 2014 by The Rosen Publishing Group, Inc.
29 East 21st Street, New York, NY 10010

Copyright © 2014 by The Rosen Publishing Group, Inc.

All rights reserved. No part of this book may be reproduced in any form without permission in writing from the publisher, except by a reviewer.

First Edition

Editor: Jennifer Way
Book Design: Greg Tucker

Photo Credits: Cover, p. 22 Photo Researchers/Getty Images; p. 5 American Stock Archives/Archive Photos/Getty Images; p. 6 Frederic Remington/The Bridgeman Art Library/Getty Images; p. 7 Buyenlarge/Archive Photos/Getty Images; p. 8 Galyna Andrushko/Shutterstock.com; pp. 10, 19, 21 MPI/Stringer/Archive Photos/Getty Images; p. 11 Richard Cummins/Lonely Planet Images/Getty Images; p. 12 Henryk Sadura/Shutterstock.com; pp. 13, 17 James L. Amos/National Geographic/Getty Images; p. 15 N. Currier/The Bridgeman Art Library/Getty Images; p. 16 David Dea/Shutterstock.com; p. 18 De Agostini Picture Library/Getty Images; p. 20 Geoffrey Clifford/The Image Bank/Getty Images.

Library of Congress Cataloging-in-Publication Data

Lynette, Rachel.
 The Oregon Trail / by Rachel Lynette. — First edition.
    pages cm. — (Pioneer spirit : the westward expansion)
 Includes index.
 ISBN 978-1-4777-0786-9 (library binding) — ISBN 978-1-4777-0905-4 (pbk.) — ISBN 978-1-4777-0906-1 (6-pack)
 1. Oregon National Historic Trail—Juvenile literature. 2. Overland journeys to the Pacific—Juvenile literature. 3. Frontier and pioneer life—West (U.S.)—Juvenile literature. 4. United States—Territorial expansion—Juvenile literature. I. Title.
 F597.L98 2014
 978'.02—dc23
                                        2013000190

Manufactured in the United States of America

CPSIA Compliance Information: Batch #S13PK5: For Further Information contact Rosen Publishing, New York, New York at 1-800-237-9932

CONTENTS

To the West!

In the early 1800s, people in the eastern and central parts of the United States wanted to travel west to settle in the Oregon **Territory**. At that time, there were no cars, trains, or airplanes. The only ways to make such a long journey were by ship or by covered wagon. Traveling around South America by ship was expensive. Most families traveled over land instead.

The route these pioneers took was called the Oregon Trail. Between 300,000 and 500,000 people made the journey west on the trail. The trail played an important role in **westward expansion** because it brought so many people west.

This photograph shows people traveling along the Oregon Trail by covered wagon. This route west was at its greatest use between 1843 and 1869.

Trailblazers

The first white people to live in the western part of North America were fur traders called mountain men. They lived in the wilderness. They trapped animals and traded the furs. They made the trails that would become the Oregon Trail. In 1824, a mountain man named Jedediah Smith found a **pass** through the Rocky Mountains. This meant that families with wagons could now travel through the mountains to Oregon.

In this painting, Jedediah Smith (left) is exploring a desert. Smith was the first white man to explore many parts of the American West, including parts of what would become the Oregon Trail.

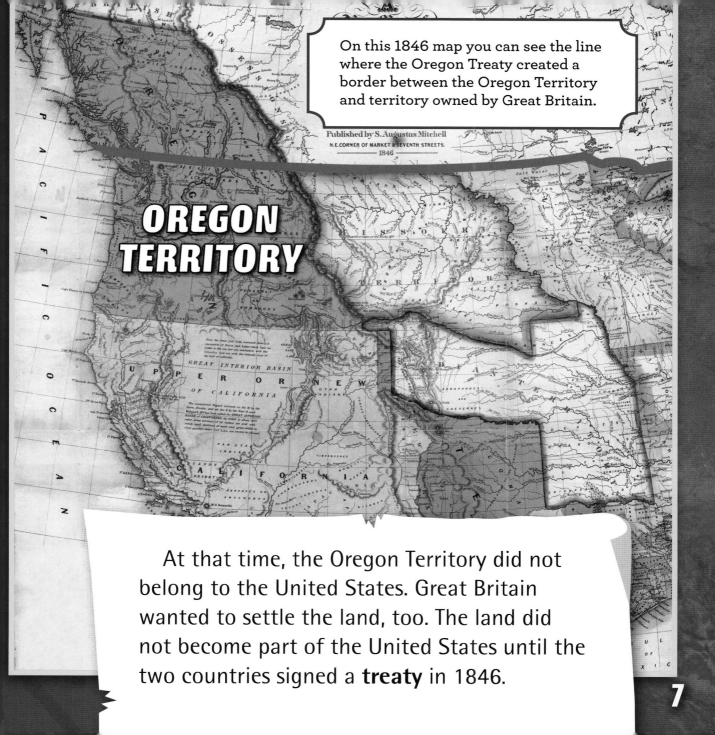

On this 1846 map you can see the line where the Oregon Treaty created a border between the Oregon Territory and territory owned by Great Britain.

Published by S. Augustus Mitchell
N.E. CORNER OF MARKET & SEVENTH STREETS.
1846

OREGON TERRITORY

At that time, the Oregon Territory did not belong to the United States. Great Britain wanted to settle the land, too. The land did not become part of the United States until the two countries signed a **treaty** in 1846.

The Great Migration

The first large group to travel the Oregon Trail left from Independence, Missouri, in May 1843. One thousand people loaded up 120 wagons for the trip.

Cascade Mountains

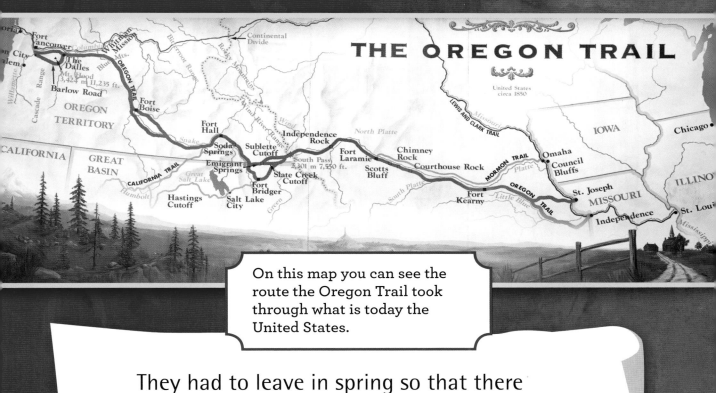

THE OREGON TRAIL

United States circa 1850

On this map you can see the route the Oregon Trail took through what is today the United States.

They had to leave in spring so that there would be grass for their **livestock** to eat along the way. They also needed to get across the Cascade Mountains before winter.

Teams of oxen pulled most of the wagons because they are strong animals. The wagons traveled in a long line called a wagon train. At night, they made the wagons into a large circle. The journey was 2,000 miles (3,219 km) long and took up to six months.

Following a Dream

The people traveling west along the Oregon Trail were called **emigrants**. Most emigrants wanted to start a new life in Oregon. They had heard the land was good for farming. Some were escaping **debts** or the law. Others were **missionaries**. They wanted to spread Christianity to the Native Americans.

The Whitman Mission, shown here, was a settlement founded by missionaries in 1836. It became a stop near the end of the Oregon Trail and is near today's Walla Walla, Washington.

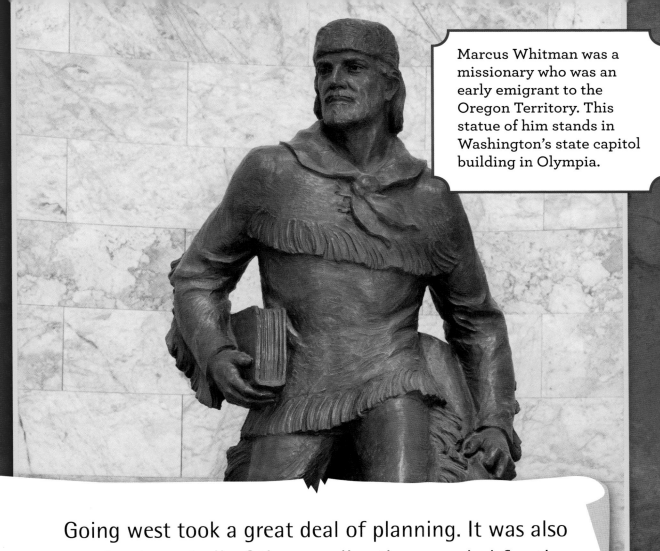

Marcus Whitman was a missionary who was an early emigrant to the Oregon Territory. This statue of him stands in Washington's state capitol building in Olympia.

Going west took a great deal of planning. It was also expensive to get all of the supplies they needed for the journey. Emigrants had to pack enough food to last for at least six months. For a family of four, that was more than 1,000 pounds (454 kg)! They also needed tools, cooking pots, medicines, and other supplies.

A Dangerous Journey

Life on the Oregon Trail was hard, dangerous, and often boring. The wagons were so full of supplies that only the very old or very sick would ride in them. Everyone else walked the 12 to 15 miles (19-24 km) that the train traveled each day.

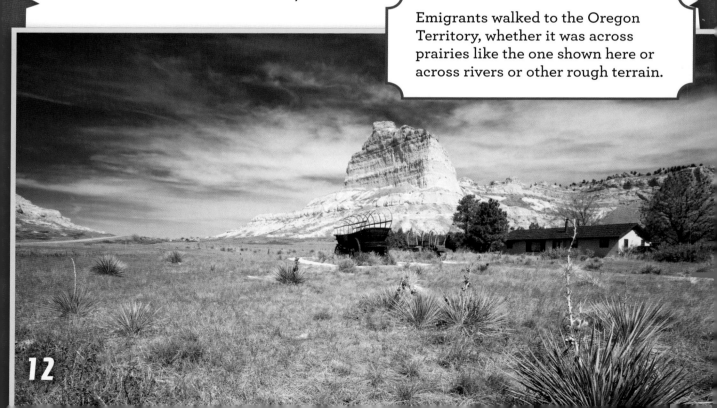

Emigrants walked to the Oregon Territory, whether it was across prairies like the one shown here or across rivers or other rough terrain.

This scientist has found the remains of an emigrant who died along the Oregon Trail in Wyoming.

Emigrants faced harsh weather that ranged from blistering heat to snowstorms. They had to take their wagons across rivers, where many lost their lives. Others were killed in accidents or by wild animals. The biggest killer was illness. Thousands of emigrants died from a **contagious** disease called **cholera**. Their bodies were buried along the trail.

Life on a Wagon Train

The days started long before sunrise on a wagon train. First, the wagon was loaded. Then, breakfast was made and eaten. After that, each wagon took its place in the long line. The train traveled all day long, taking only a short break for lunch.

As soon as the wagons stopped for the night, the children went to find firewood. When there was no wood, they burned dried buffalo **dung**. Women made dinner. Meals were usually made up of foods like bacon, beans, and bread. Men made repairs and sometimes went hunting. After dinner, families often got together to play music or tell stories before bed.

This picture shows emigrants in a wagon train near the Rocky Mountains. People hunted or gathered wood as the train made its daily journey.

Native Americans

Many emigrants were afraid of being attacked by Native Americans on the Oregon Trail. This did not happen very often, though. Most Native Americans allowed the wagon trains to pass peacefully. Often, Native Americans came to trade with the emigrants and sometimes to help.

Buffalo

This painting shows emigrants on the Oregon Trail passing by a group of Native Americans. As more emigrants moved into the West, the relationship between settlers and Native Americans worsened.

Even though the Native Americans lived in North America first, the emigrants did not think that the land belonged to them. They hunted the buffalo that the Indians needed to live. They spread diseases that killed thousands of Native Americans. By 1860, many Native Americans were no longer friendly to the emigrants.

River or Road?

After months of traveling through grassy plains, dry deserts, and steep mountains, the emigrants finally reached the Columbia River in Oregon. Now they had a choice. They could either float down the river or take the Barlow Road over Mount Hood. Both choices could be dangerous. The river was rough, and many boats overturned. The road was almost too steep for the wagons.

Oregon City, Oregon, was the last stop on the Oregon Trail. This photograph shows what the city looked like in 1857.

This painting shows emigrants on the Barlow Road, near Mount Hood, in Oregon.

Once they arrived in Oregon's Willamette Valley, most emigrants were glad they had come. The land was good for farming, and the government granted 640 acres (259 ha) of land to each adult male. Families then built cabins and began their new lives.

End of an Era

Not everyone took the Oregon Trail all the way to Oregon. In 1848, when gold was discovered near San Francisco in California, many took the southwest branch of the trail to California where they hoped to strike it rich. Many **Mormons** took a branch called the Mormon Trail to Utah after being forced out of their homes in Illinois and Iowa.

Today there are stone trail markers to show the Oregon Trail's route. This marker is in Wyoming.

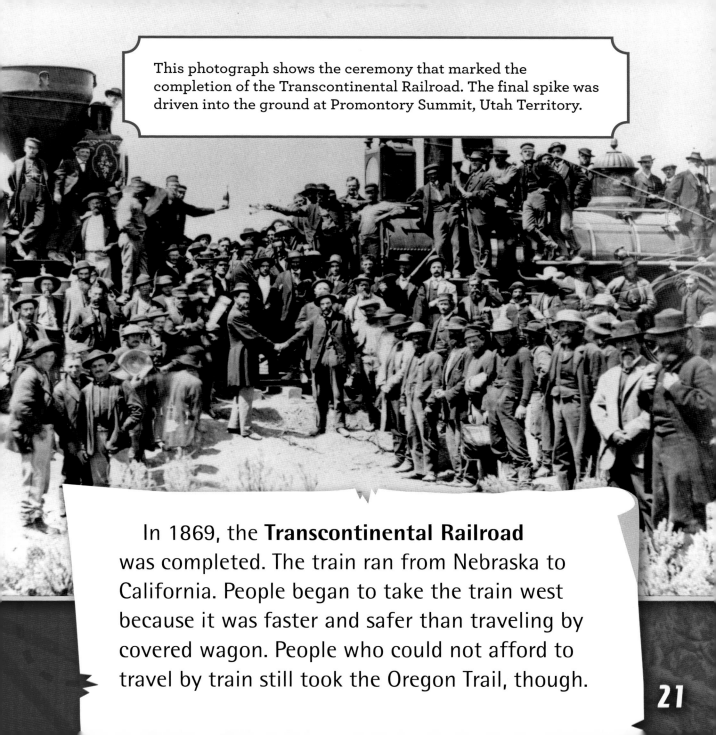

This photograph shows the ceremony that marked the completion of the Transcontinental Railroad. The final spike was driven into the ground at Promontory Summit, Utah Territory.

In 1869, the **Transcontinental Railroad** was completed. The train ran from Nebraska to California. People began to take the train west because it was faster and safer than traveling by covered wagon. People who could not afford to travel by train still took the Oregon Trail, though.

An Important Trail

About one out of every ten people who started on the Oregon Trail died along the way. However, those who made it played an important part in westward expansion. The Oregon Trail brought thousands of people to settle in the West. The land the Oregon Trail passed through became part of several new states. Oregon became a state in 1859, Washington and Montana in 1889, and Idaho and Wyoming in 1890.

After the Transcontinental Railroad was completed, people could make the journey west in about a week instead of six months. This slowed the use of the Oregon Trail, although the westward expansion continued.

GLOSSARY

cholera (KAH-luh-rah) A painful illness of the stomach that causes cramping and vomiting.

contagious (kun-TAY-jus) Able to be passed on.

debts (DETS) Things that are owed.

dung (DUNG) Animal waste.

emigrants (EM-uh-grints) People who left a place to settle somewhere else.

livestock (LYV-stok) Animals raised by people.

missionaries (MIH-shuh-ner-eez) People who go to another place to tell people about a certain faith.

Mormons (MOR-munz) Members of a church that was founded in the United States by Joseph Smith in 1830.

pass (PAS) A path through the mountains.

territory (TER-uh-tor-ee) Land that is controlled by a person or a group of people.

transcontinental railroad (trants-kon-tuh-NEN-tul RAYL-rohd) The train system that crossed the United States in the late 1800s.

treaty (TREE-tee) An official agreement, signed and agreed upon by each party.

westward expansion (WES-twurd ik-SPANT-shun) The continued growth of the United States by adding land to the west and having settlers move onto it.

INDEX

WEBSITES

Due to the changing nature of Internet links, PowerKids Press has developed an online list of websites related to the subject of this book. This site is updated regularly. Please use this link to access the list: www.powerkidslinks.com/pswe/trail/

J 978 LYNETTE

Lynette, Rachel.
The Oregon Trail

R4002772352   SOF

SOUTH FULTON BRANCH
Atlanta-Fulton Public Library